AF413225

The Power of Words

WORDS AND THEIR SIDE-EFFECTS

LORAN JOLY

Contents

Introduction

The author does not subscribe entirely to all of the views of people mentioned in this book.

Instead, he is an eclectic, who has found himself creating his own cookbook of ideas.

As per the idea mentioned in the movie "No Reservations", where an analyst had stated his view that the best recipes are the ones we create ourselves.

Or put another way, focusing on the best, and putting the rest on the back burner.

***

To do these things, he found his having studied electrical engineering at West Point, and four years at the half-load level at Berea College, starting at the age of forty-one – where he took fifteen mathematics classes – and used spaced repetition software, too, for fifteen years – to be crucial to examining and growing his views on words, as well as creating ones for himself.

Preface

This is what one might call a White Paper, or Musing, too, or Rough Draft, ...

And thus, is not Polished; or Utterly-Complete; and too, of course, both a Hypothesis and is Subject to Revision and Change of Mind.

YET, PUT OUT in UN-Polished FORM, DUE to ...

The probability of a car accident, or stroke, or heart attack, or cancer, or Alzheimers' striking the author.

As well as the importance of this topic, and in view of all the other writings that this author already has "piled up", ready to press the print button on, almost literally.

And to high level of "content" – generating, overall.

CHAPTER ONE

Martin Luther, the Reformation, and the printing press

We have all heard, the phrase "The power of the pen"....

For instance, Martin Luther is said to have utilized The Power of the Pen: and he could not have made an impact in the world, in this way, until the Gutenberg printing press – a form of pen.

Yet, has our language evolved at the same rate as technology, making of money, or feeling creature comforts in the physical sense?

For, too, we have reached the moon, and likely, Mars, too: but what of our Vocabulary?

Does our Vocabulary need a Moonshot Project?

***

Now, we might consider these articles:

"7 Ways the Printing Press Changed the World"

"In the 15th century, an innovation enabled people to share knowledge more quickly and widely. Civilization never looked back."

BY: DAVE ROOS UPDATED: MARCH 27, 2023 | ORIGINAL: AUGUST 28, 2019

https://www.history.com/news/print-
ing-press-renaissance

***

"The Importance of the Printing Press for the Protestant Reformation, Part One":

https://www.reformation21.org/arti-
cles/the-importance-of-the-printing.php

"The Importance of the Printing Press for the Protestant Reformation, Part Two":

https://www.reformation21.org/articles/the-importance-of-the-printing-press-for-the-protestant-reformation-part-two.php

CHAPTER TWO

Is Hate a big issue, or is Hate based on Disrespect?

Now, these days, what with Independent publishing, some say that we have gotten yet further past some Gatekeepers, some might say, and can reach more Democratically than ever before.

***

Yet, at the same time, when does this become a problem, too?

For what is meant by "hate speech"?

Indeed, do we want to see everyone using freedom of speech in ways we would never think of doing with physical aggression?

Ought we to have no views on analogs to freedom of The Fist or freedom of The Gun?

Of course, aren't there too many laws already, on the other hand?

***

I think we might want to ponder the words in this video by Arnold Schwarzenegger:

"Arnold Schwarzenegger has a powerful message for those who have gone down a path of hate."

https://www.youtube.com/watch?v=XYn5t0tu-uAk&pp=ygUaYXJub2xkIHNjaHdhcnplbmVnZ2VyIGhhdGU%3D

***

And secondly, might we ponder this video too?

"Why do some movements succeed, while others fail? | Greg Satell | TEDxMorristown"

https://youtu.be/IOt1dLVyHjQ

Chapter Three

Does The Pen Write With Radioactive Ink?

But, does The Pen have radioactive ink – or is the ink non-toxic?

***

For haven't we heard, too,

"I sure Stuck My Foot in my Mouth" that time?

Or, too,

"It's not What you said, it's HOW you SAID it".

(What WORDS were used....)

Or, as one might say,

"I STUCK my PEN in my Mouth again!"

"And it caused a blaze!"

collage by author & images from Canva

So, might this pen say some truths, and at the same time, use some words that are the equivalent of a germ?

image by Canva

In other words, do some of the words that The Pen writes, "have COVID"?

Or, are our pens "smelling", and we don't know it, rather like going out camping for two weeks and then going to a job interview two hours after
returning to town, and forgetting to take a shower, only to wonder, after the interview, why the interviewer was grimacing and never called us back?

Our words have great impact

Consider this powerful video:

The Power of Not Reacting | Stop Overreacting | How to Control Your Emotions

(Dr. Levry)

https://www.youtube.com/watch?v=mhZalV4PRbo&pp=ygUiZHIgbGV2cnkgdGhlIHBvd2VyIG9mIG5vdCByZWFjdGluZw%3D%3D

Profound videos on Word communication and An Alternative Way

I believe that a fundamental issue with our words, is the dual meaning that most all of our "People-Words" have, in fact:

For our words about people convey several meanings: not just what "IS", but how "It" ORIGINATED, and ITS FUTURE, too.

***

A most interesting video might be seen, here, by the way:

The Hidden Power Of Words":

(Sehnend YouTube channel)

https://youtu.be/sUjBt328Tx8

***

Alternatively, to use no words at all might also be advantageous, as this same YouTube creator points out in a profound video:

The Art of Unspoken Impact: Influencing Others Without Speaking

https://youtu.be/DgLmxvgDdjo

CHAPTER SIX

Thinking as discussed by Cognitive Therapists

Now, Cognitive Therapy talks of the importance of our thinking, and how critically tied it is, to our "moods" – our happiness, I think we could say.

And there is talk, then, of incorrect Core Beliefs.

***

But how well is Cognitive Therapy able to state, plain and simple, what Core Beliefs are causing our problems – and with great clarity?

Without Stepping on some Big Toes?

***

As one physician stated to me fifteen years ago, about the psychoanalysis I had participated in, forty years ago:

"I'll just TELL you WHAT you need to know".....

[But he didn't, exactly....]

***

Furthermore, I know of no psychologist or psychoanalyst who has written a dictionary of Words by which to not be "Thinking with Cognitively-Distorted" words.

***

Perhaps this is part of why some clinics have banners on their bulletin boards, advertising the latest meditation or Mindfulness Meditation workshops that are being held?

image from Canva

***

Indeed, some say we "Think too much"....

Yet, on the other hand, some urge us to think more:

"Think and Grow Rich", by Napoleon Hill.

***

But, thinking with which WORDS?

For, as it has been said in Alcoholics Anonymous meetings,

"You have 'STINKING THINKING"...

Or, perhaps I would say, too,

"We all tend to have some STINKING WORDS we use...."

CHAPTER SEVEN

The Buddhist Approach to Thinking – and Words, too?

So, given a great lack of good words to use when it comes to talking of us human beings, I'm not at all surprised at our state on the planet.

And the response of some, to "Think Less".

Or, "You are Overanalyzing things"

Or finally, the words of the monk, Ajahn Brahm, who talks of how, in his view – schooled as a physicist, by the way, at Camibridge University, once upon a time –

he claims that the only people who would benefit from more thinking, are those who are "Enlightened" – whatever that word might mean.

***

> *I would, in fact, step out on a bit of a new realm and suggest that such "Enlightenment" would basically mean the* **CONDITION of HAVING a LARGE SET of**
>
> **"ENLIGHTENED WORDS"**

I say this, based upon having attended a hundred sessions of meditation every Saturday for two years, around

2015, and also having attended lectures and seminars at a Buddhist monastery, last year, and having also talked with two of the Buddhist Tibetan monks, there, too.

***

Consider the words of the profound monk in Australia, Ajahn Brahm, in June 2022:

"Thinking gets in the way of meditation"...

(49' 18" point in the video):
https://www.youtube.com/live/0Z8q_FWbWa8?si=4rnCGCH03AtH3SO0&t=2958
As part of his talk,
"Expectations Cause Suffering | Ajahn Brahm | 24 June 2022")

Link below for the entire video:

https://www.youtube.com/live/0Z8q_FWbWa8?si=
0cyumFlDHuW97aly

The words of a Psychologist on Disrespectful words and non-verbal communications in relationships between two partners

Now, for a perhaps challenging view for some, there is a most interesting view on the role of

DISRESPECT – which I believe to be at the core of our communication difficulties, including talk via The Pen....

For,

In a video, Dr. Orion Taraban talks of what he calls the one "Unbreakable Rule", when it comes to women relating with men.

This rather thought-provoking, if not tweaking-to-some, video, likely has large kernels of truth for all of us, including our words as a part of the ink of The Pen concept:

"How to get any MAN you WANT: The UNBREAKABLE RULE"

https://youtu.be/qKlgl_98uzI

"In this episode, I discuss the third -- and final -- consideration for getting any man you want. If a woman has proven herself both functionally useful and sexually exciting, and she still hasn't been able to retain a desired relationship, in most cases it is because she has violated the unbreakable rule, namely: she has been difficult and disrespectful. Under no circumstances, can a woman allow herself to disrespect the man she wants. No exceptions."

Presented by Orion Taraban, Psy.D. PsycHacks provides viewers with a brief, thought-provoking video several days a week on a variety of psychological topics, inspired by his clinical practice. The intention is for the core idea contained within each video to inspire viewers to see something about themselves or their world in a slightly different light. The ultimate mission of the channel is to reduce the amount of unnecessary suffering in the world.

The words of Abraham Lincoln resulted in being challenged to a duel

Abraham Lincoln "Stuck his Pen in His Mouth" in a rather difficult way, some would say...

As I first read about, in Dale Carnegie's book, "How to Win Friends and Influence People".

And there is mention elsewhere, too:

For, Abraham Lincoln was once challenged to a duel....

collage by author - images by Canva

Question: Did Lincoln ever fight a duel?

https://www.lincolncollection.org/discover/ask-an-expert/qa-archive/did-lincoln-ever-fight-a-duel/

Lincoln — What Sparked Lincoln's Duel & His Unusual Fight Terms

https://www.donnajanellbowman.com/2018/01/03/what-sparked-lincolns-duel-his-unusual-terms/

Napoleon Hill on words

Napoleon Hill has stated some key things about words, too:"Napoleon Hill - 10 Rules of Self Discipline YOU MUST SEE"

"Napoleon Hill - 10 Rules of Self Discipline YOU MUST SEE"

https://youtu.be/nZ5CXiMgOCw

Tony Robbins has a key chapter on words

Tony Robbins has a key chapter on words in his book, Awaken the Giant Within".

Chapter 9 is entitled "The Vocabulary of Ultimate Success".

Immigrant and Farm Influence on the Author's View on Words and Communicating in General

The author's views on words and interaction are colored by his upbringing, including his mother, in the photo, below, as in Poland in 1940 during World War II, and later a war refugee to Ellis Island in 1950.

What is also of interest, perhaps, is that his grandmother raised him – she in the center of the image below, taken in 1940 – raised him during the waking hours of his first four years of life, and he also spent all his childhood years on her farm, where he left the farm only once or twice a week. Indeed, she never drove a car, and both his mother and grandmother came to America – Ellis Island – knowing no English.

Indeed, the only books his grandmother ever read were the bible and a few large-print Reader's Digest condensed books".

And his grandmother and he never spoke scarcely a word between themselves, then, until he was thirty....

Furthermore, the author spent a year, after Kindergarten – a black Kindergarten in inner-city Detroit – the "ghettos" – largely in the woods of North Carolina, hiking, collecting turtles, crayfish, and leaves and rocks.

And his father – still alive currently – had been a "high school dropout" at seventeen – after departing home at age ten – and later attained a Ph.D. degree in English literature at a well-known University....

So, all of this to be taken into account, regarding the author's interest in words....

*Photograph
of my
mother, left,
at the age of
two; my
grandmoth-
er, center,
and a
helper,
right, 1940,
as war
refugees in
Poland,
during
World War
II*

And, my summers at my European relatives' farm in Michigan, during my childhood years...

Great-grandmother stayed on the farm for a while – as seen in the background – and the author's mother, bottom right – author, bottom left....

*Author's great-grandmother, in back-
ground; mother, right, and myself, left
at the age of about seven*

author, left; mother, center; sister, right,

on farm in 1960s

Dedication

To my parents, who made this possible.

For instance, my mother, an immigrant from eastern Poland, having come to America at the age of twelve, after a two week long boat journey, to Ellis Island....

*My mother as a young gal in Europe, before
coming to America*

And to my father, too, a most astute Trainer in life....

Brought up in the ghettos of Philadelphia; left school
at the age of seventeen; and later acquired a GED and

went on to obtain a Ph.D. degree at a major University in English Literature; who thus led to my interest and pursuit of writing at a very early age; and too, with respect to his love of photography, both of these areas, too, rubbing off on me: hence, "The apple doesn't fall far from the tree"?

Then, too, my grandparents:

For significantly, my grandmother raised me during my first four years, in my waking hours. And her husband – my grandfather – worked in the tool and die industry for cars; she, born in eastern Poland, like my mother, and was a farmer there; he, born in Odessa, Ukraine, and a Mennonite, and herb-collector and maker of many grandfather clocks in his spare time, on their farm in Michigan:

Grandparents in Niagara Falls, I
believe

And to my farm experience, as a youth, each summer, in Michigan:

About the Author

The author resides in Kentucky,

The author does not have a Ph.D. or an MD degree. Nor is he a college graduate – for he does not consider his four years at West Point to be a college, and his four years at Berea College, studying solely athematics, were as a community member at the half time level, and no degree was ever thus awarded....

***

These are some of his credentials....

The author's influences include ...

Key aspects of the author's life have included...

Last day at West Point in 1983

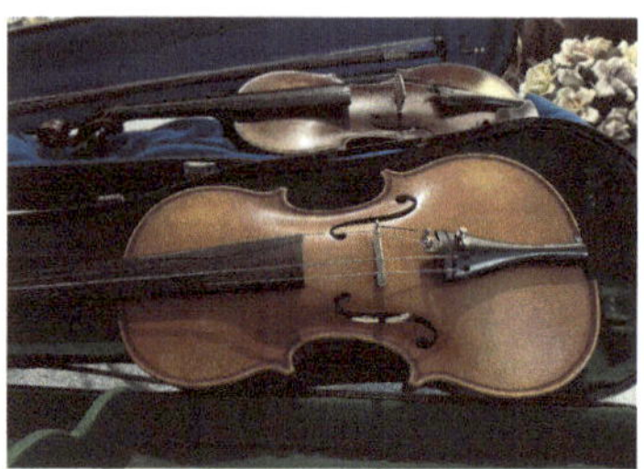

My violins: the closest one was purchased and carried on my father's back as he traveled in Germany. I started Suzuki violin lessons in North Carolina at the age of seven, and later studied at The MacPhail Center For Music in Minneapolis, Minnesota, when our family moved there in 1970 when I was ten; in eleventh grade, I played in a local college orchestra, and in my senior year, I took violin lessons at the University of Kentucky from a violin professor, and played in the Central Kentucky Youth Symphony Orchestra, practicing my violin at home, two hours a day, seven days a week.

Refund policy

REFUND INFORMATION

Desire a refund? No problem: 100% refund, for any reason at all, and absolutely no questions asked, period. And no time limit on this offer. I recognize that sometimes, purchased items are discovered to simply not be a "good fit", or for any number of other reasons...

Loran Joly

If for any reason you desire a refund or desire to leave a comment,

please contact me at:

message@goldpogo.com

or

ReEnvision Press
Box #1036
1303 US 127 South
Suite 104
Frankfort, KY 40601